Contents

The lifecycle of
birth and reproduction

The birth of a new person is one of the most extraordinary things that can happen. Every minute, around the world, about 250 babies are born – that's more than four a second!

Sperm and an egg

These male sperm are swarming around a female egg. The fusion of a sperm and an egg is called fertilisation (see pages 12–13).

Reproductive organs

Men and women make a baby together by a process called sexual reproduction. A man and a woman have different reproductive organs that make up the male and female reproductive systems. They only become fully functional when people reach puberty in their early teens.

New born

This baby is one of many born throughout the world. Birth is one of the first stages in a person's life.

Sex cells

The male and female reproductive systems produce special sex cells. Men's sex cells are called sperm and women's sex cells are called eggs. These cells carry information from the person who produced them in the form of genes. Genes are chemical codes that shape the way a person looks and functions. A sperm and an egg fuse together inside a woman in a process called fertilisation. If this happens, a new person starts to develop.

The gift of life

After about 38–40 weeks of growth inside its mother a new baby is ready to be born. Birth is, however, only the first chapter in the story of a life. Many more changes take place as a baby grows and becomes an adult. Eventually, all people must age and die, but the process of reproduction allows them to pass on their genes to the next generation.

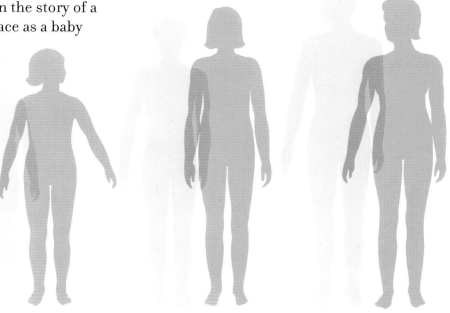

Growing up

As we grow and develop we get older and continue to change (see pages 24–29). Eventually we will die, but before that happens many of us will be able to reproduce.

THE HUMAN RACE

By 2000 there were over six billion people alive. The world's population grew rapidly in the 20th century – doubling since 1950. This massive growth was mainly due to improved health conditions, which meant that fewer babies died and people began to live for longer.

Projections for the first half of the 21st century show that the world's population will rise to around 7–10 billion by 2050. However, soon after this it should stop growing. This should happen as people get better education, a better quality of life and more access to contraceptives (see page 13) that allow them to plan the number of children they have.

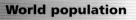

World population

These people are just some of over six billion that live on Earth today.

The female reproductive system is
where a baby grows

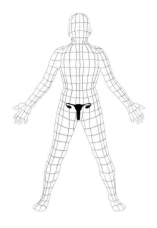

The female reproductive system lies inside a woman's body, between her hips. It is where the female sex cells, or eggs, are stored and where an egg and a sperm fuse, starting the development of a baby. The female reproductive system also protects and feeds the developing baby until it is ready to be born.

Ovaries and eggs

The ovaries are two small organs about the size of plums. They produce and store eggs. Every girl has about two million unripe eggs when she is born – her lifetime's supply. The eggs remain unripe until the girl reaches puberty in her early teens, when one egg ripens approximately every **28** days and is released (see pages **8–9**).

Reproductive organs

The ovaries, Fallopian tubes, uterus and vagina form the major parts of the female reproductive system.

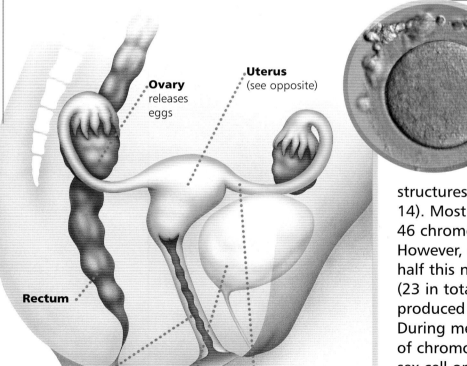

Ovary
releases
eggs

Uterus
(see opposite)

Rectum

Vagina
(see opposite)

Bladder
stores urine

Fallopian tube
is one of the
two tubes that
connect the
ovaries to
the uterus

Female egg

Eggs are the largest cells in a woman's body. However, they are still tiny, no more than 0.1 mm in diameter.

EGGS

Chromosomes are microscopic thread-like structures that carry genes (see page 14). Most cells in the body contain 46 chromosomes (in 23 pairs). However, eggs (and sperm) contain half this number of chromosomes (23 in total). These sex cells are produced by a process called meiosis. During meiosis, the 'normal' 23 pairs of chromosomes are split. Each new sex cell only gets one chromosome from each pair. When an egg fuses with a sperm the number of chromosomes returns to 46.

Fallopian tubes

When an egg is released from an ovary it enters one of two Fallopian tubes (also called oviducts or uterine tubes). The Fallopian tubes are lined with tiny hair-like cilia which move the egg along. The egg may fuse with a sperm and be fertilised as it travels down the Fallopian tube (see pages 12–13).

Inside a Fallopian tube

The walls of the Fallopian tubes are lined by tiny hair-like cilia. These move backwards and forwards rhythmically and move an egg along its journey to the uterus.

Uterus and vagina

This is a section through the central and lower part of the female reproductive system.

Uterus
supports the growth of a fertilised egg

Cervix
the lower part of the uterus that connects to the vagina

Vagina
the tube that connects the uterus to the outside of the body and receives the penis during sexual intercourse

Uterus

The uterus is a pear-shaped hollow organ that is connected to the ovaries by the Fallopian tubes. It has a special lining that can support a fertilised egg so that it grows into a new baby (see pages **18–19**). At the bottom of the uterus is an opening called the cervix, which leads to the vagina.

Vagina

The vagina is a muscular tube that connects the uterus to the outside of a woman's body. It is the passage through which sperm get into a woman's body and through which a new baby is born into the world.

Ovulation occurs during
the menstrual cycle

After a girl reaches puberty, her reproductive system goes through a series of changes that are repeated roughly every 28 days (although the cycle can be longer or shorter). These changes are called the menstrual cycle. It usually begins between the ages of 11 and 14, but can occur earlier or later.

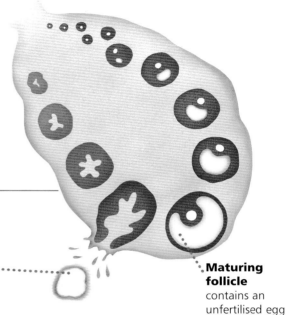

An ovary

A mature follicle in an ovary releases an egg at ovulation.

Egg release ....
begins the egg's journey from the ovary down the Fallopian tube

Maturing follicle
contains an unfertilised egg

Hormones

During the menstrual cycle the old lining of the uterus breaks down. The blood and tissue it was made of trickles out of the uterus through the vagina. This is known as a period (see opposite). Then, after about six days, a chemical messenger in the blood, called a hormone, causes an egg in one of the ovaries to begin to ripen inside a bag called a follicle. This hormone is produced by the pituitary gland, which lies just below the brain. At the same time, hormones produced by the ovaries cause the lining of the uterus to get thicker once again.

Ovulation

In another eight days the egg is mature and bursts out of its follicle. This is called ovulation. The egg leaves the ovary and is moved down the Fallopian tube where it may be fertilised if it fuses with a sperm. After ovulation, the lining of the uterus thickens further and its blood supply increases in preparation to receive a fertilised egg.

Release of hormones

*Young women like these have periods because their bodies produce special hormones that trigger the release of eggs from their ovaries. Hormones also control the other changes that occur during puberty (see pages **26–27**).*

NATURAL PROCESS

A girl's first period is a sign that she is physically able to have children and is becoming an adult. The 'bleeding' that accompanies a period is completely natural. Some women also experience aches and pains in their abdomen or back while others feel fine. These feelings are due to the physical and hormonal changes that are happening in the body.

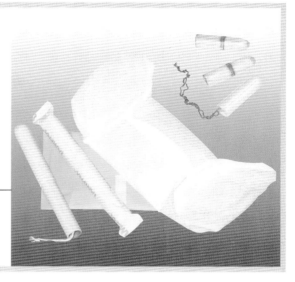

Sanitary products

Sanitary products include tampons (placed inside the vagina) and sanitary pads (worn inside underwear).

1.

An egg
develops in a follicle inside one of the ovaries

Uterus lining
breaks down

Entering the uterus

If a fertilised egg does reach the uterus, it sinks into the lining and starts to develop. The menstrual cycle then stops until after the baby is born. If fertilisation does not occur, the lining of the uterus begins to break down. The lining and the unfertilised egg pass through the uterus and out of the vagina. The menstrual cycle repeats itself after an average of 28 days.

2.

A mature egg
is released at ovulation and moved down the Fallopian tube

Uterus lining
thickens

Uterus lining
reaches full thickness in preparation for receiving a fertilised egg

3.

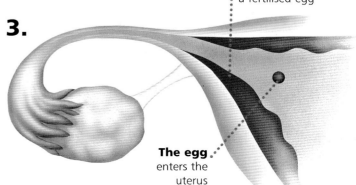

The egg
enters the uterus

The reproductive cycle

1. Days 1–5: The lining of the uterus breaks down and flows out through the vagina (a period). Inside each ovary, eggs continue to develop.
2. Days 6–17: A follicle matures and releases an egg down a Fallopian tube. The lining of the uterus thickens.
3. Days 18–28: The lining of the uterus continues to thicken. The egg enters the uterus. If it has been fertilised the egg implants in the lining; if not, it passes out of the vagina, beginning another cycle.

The male reproductive system
produces sperm

The male reproductive system manufactures sperm in the testes. Sperm leave a man's body through his penis.

Sperm production

Sperm are produced in the testes when a boy reaches puberty (around **13** years old). The testes (also called testicles) are two oval-shaped organs that hang outside the body in a sac of skin called the scrotum. The testes lie outside the body because sperm production takes place best at a slightly lower temperature (**34** to **36** degrees Celsius) than normal body temperature (**37** degrees Celsius).

A sperm

*Sperm, like this one, are about **0.05** mm long — half the size of a female egg.*

Male hormones

*Male hormones produced at puberty make boys, like these, start to produce sperm (see pages **26–27**).*

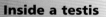

Epididymis
is a tightly coiled tube where sperm mature

Inside a testis

Sperm are produced in the seminiferous tubules inside the testes (see opposite). The sperm then go to the epididymis where they mature.

Sperm preparation

Sperm mature in the epididymis, which is a coiled tube that runs round the edge of each testis. During sexual intercourse sperm are carried into the body in two tubes. Sperm are mixed with nutrient-rich fluids produced by the prostate gland and seminal vesicles to produce semen. The urethra carries semen out of the body. It runs through the centre of the penis and also carries urine from the bladder.

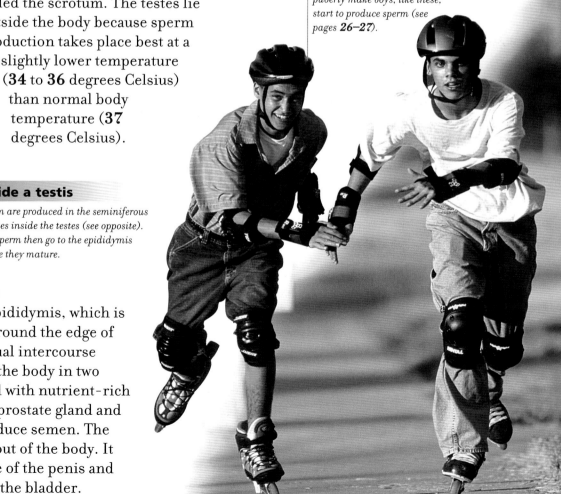

SPERM

Sperm are male sex cells – only about 0.05 millimetres long. They look like tadpoles with a head, and a long tail which can move to propel them along. Every day about 100 million immature sperm are produced inside tiny tubes, called seminiferous tubules, that fill the testes. New sperm are made continuously from when a boy reaches puberty until old age, although the number of sperm produced declines as he gets older.

Millions of sperm

These sperm are in a seminiferous tubule. Sperm develop from cells in the testes. Sperm that are not carried away, for example during sexual intercourse, are broken down and recycled.

Penis

The penis is a tube-shaped organ that hangs outside the body. When a man is sexually stimulated, the spongy tissue inside the penis fills with blood, making it larger and stiffer. This is called an erection. It enables the man to put his penis into his partner's vagina so that sperm can be transferred into her vagina.

Reproductive organs

The male reproductive system is designed to produce and store sperm and to release it during sexual intercourse so that a female egg can be fertilised.

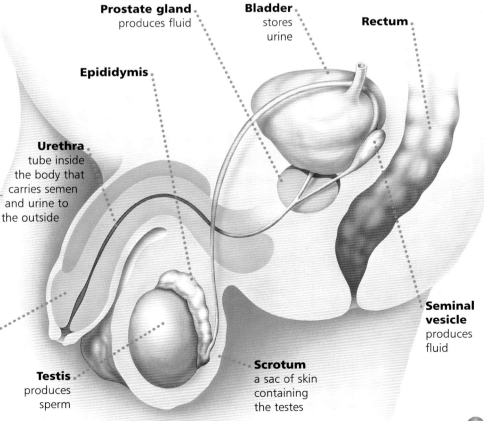

Prostate gland
produces fluid

Bladder
stores urine

Rectum

Epididymis

Urethra
tube inside the body that carries semen and urine to the outside

Seminal vesicle
produces fluid

Penis
carries sperm into a woman's vagina when erect during sexual intercourse

Testis
produces sperm

Scrotum
a sac of skin containing the testes

Fertilisation occurs after
sexual intercourse

The first stage in the creation of a new life is the production of sperm and eggs. The next stage happens when an egg and a sperm meet and fertilisation takes place. Fertilisation is the process by which the nucleus of a sperm and an egg fuse together and a new baby starts to develop.

Sexual intercourse

The process of fertilisation starts during sexual intercourse. This is a very intimate and special act between a man and a woman in which a man's erect penis is placed inside a woman's vagina. The two people then move so that the man's penis is stimulated further. This results in a reflex action, called ejaculation, that causes muscles along the sperm ducts to contract and sperm to be released into the vagina.

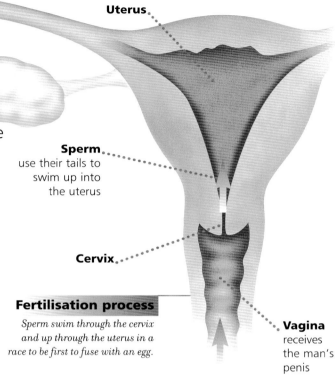

Uterus

Sperm
use their tails to swim up into the uterus

Cervix

Vagina
receives the man's penis

Fertilisation process

Sperm swim through the cervix and up through the uterus in a race to be first to fuse with an egg.

Long journey

Millions of sperm enter the vagina when a man ejaculates. These sperm travel up through the cervix and into the uterus by moving their tails. They are also carried along by muscular contractions in the uterus. Less than a thousand sperm eventually survive to enter the woman's fallopian tubes – a journey that takes about five hours.

Making love

Sexual intercourse is sometimes called 'making love' because it is a special part of a relationship between a man and a woman.

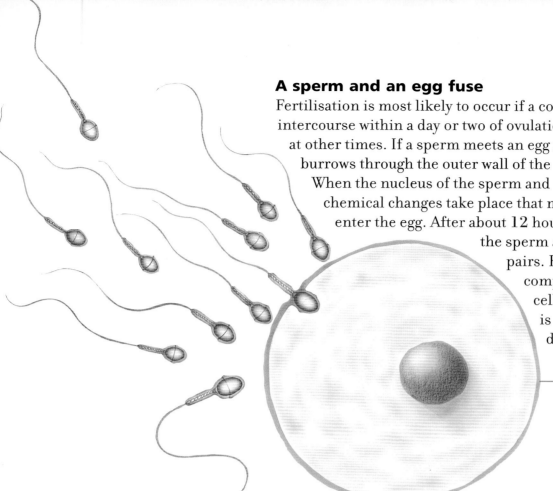

A sperm and an egg fuse

Fertilisation is most likely to occur if a couple have sexual intercourse within a day or two of ovulation, although it can occur at other times. If a sperm meets an egg in the fallopian tube it burrows through the outer wall of the egg and loses its tail. When the nucleus of the sperm and egg fuse together, chemical changes take place that mean no other sperm can enter the egg. After about 12 hours the chromosomes in the sperm and egg join up into pairs. Fertilisation is then complete and the first new cell of a potential new baby is ready to start developing.

Breaking through

Of all the millions of sperm released, only one can finally break through the wall of the egg and fuse with its nucleus.

CONTRACEPTION

Many couples want to plan when and if they have children. To do this they control whether fertilisation takes place by using devices called contraceptives. They are available in many forms, but include condoms (worn over the penis and inside the vagina) and caps (worn over the cervix). Both devices stop sperm entering the uterus. Contraceptive pills, patches and injections work by stopping ovulation, and IUCDs (Intrauterine Contraceptive Devices) stop a fertilised egg implanting in the wall of the uterus.

Controlling pregnancies

Today, couples can choose from a variety of contraceptive devices including condoms, caps and pills.

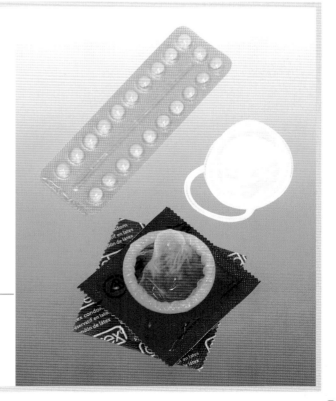

A baby is a mixture of
genetic information

When a sperm and an egg fuse the genetic information they contain joins together as well. The way this information is organised shapes what the new baby will eventually look like.

Genes

Because sperm and eggs have 23 chromosomes each (see page 6), the new cell they form has 46 chromosomes. These chromosomes are arranged in pairs. One chromosome in each pair comes from the mother's egg cell and the other comes from the father's sperm cell. Each pair of chromosomes has genes positioned on it at specific locations. The way these genes are paired affects the functioning and appearance of the new baby, for example its eye colour.

A human body cell

*The fusion of a sperm and an egg nucleus forms a single human cell. It contains **46** chromosomes.*

Nucleus
contains the chromosomes

Human chromosomes

Chromosomes are arranged in pairs. Each pair contains a unique combination of genetic information — the instructions for the creation of a new human being.

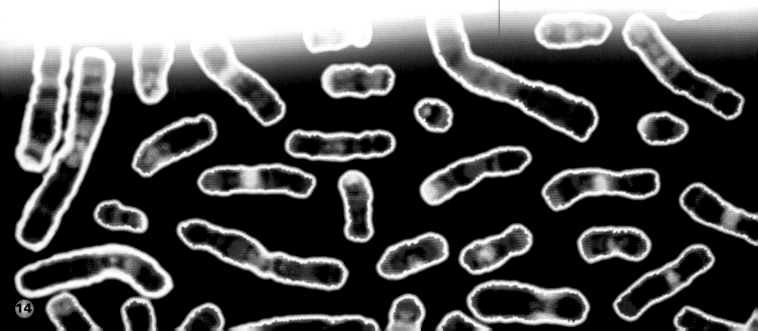

Inheriting characteristics

Genes give instructions. If a baby inherits genes from the mother and the father that give the instruction 'blue eyes', then the baby will have blue eyes (see right, 1). But if one of the 'eye colour' pair of genes gives the instruction 'blue eyes' and the other 'brown eyes', then he or she will have brown eyes (2, 3 and 4). This is because the genetic instruction for brown eyes is dominant and always affects a person's appearance. The instruction for blue eyes affects a person's appearance only if it is part of a matching pair. The passing on of characteristics from one generation to another is called heredity.

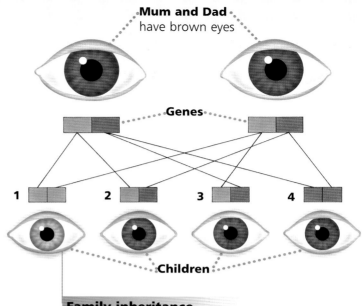

Mum and Dad have brown eyes

Genes

1 2 3 4

Children

Family inheritance

Even though both parents have brown eyes, they have one blue and one brown gene. However, the genetic instruction for brown eyes is dominant. Therefore, for a child to have blue eyes, the instruction for blue eyes must come from both parents (1).

BOY OR GIRL?

The gender, or sex, of a new baby – whether it is a boy or girl – is decided by the genes the baby receives from its father.

The genes for sex are carried on a special pair of sex chromosomes. Sex chromosomes are called X and Y because of their shape. Someone with a pair of X chromosomes is female. Someone with an X and a Y chromosome is male.

Sperm and eggs have one sex chromosome each. Eggs have an X sex chromosome only. Half of all sperm have an X chromosome and half have a Y. This means that the sex of the baby is decided by the sex chromosome in the sperm; the chances of it being a boy or a girl are 50:50.

Unique people

Each sperm and egg contains a selection of the genetic information from the person it came from. When their nuclei fuse a unique person is produced. This is why the children from the same parents can be very different.

Four generations

The characteristics of these members of the same family are similar, but also different. We each inherit a unique selection of our parents' genes.

The cell divides on its **journey to the uterus**

After fertilisation the first cell of the new baby is moved down the Fallopian tube. The cell divides, first into two cells, then four, then eight cells and so on. This is the start of the process of cell division.

Cell division

Each time the cells of the developing baby divide, the genetic information inside them is copied – each new cell contains exactly the same information as the one it came from. This type of cell division is called mitosis. Almost all cells in the body are made by mitosis, except for sperm and eggs.

Building blocks

This cell has divided into the first cells of a new human being.

72 hours after fertilisation
the first cell has become a ball of 16 cells called a morula

Twelve hours after fertilisation
the nucleus of the sperm and egg have joined together

30 hours after fertilisation
the single cell has divided into two cells

Mitosis

*During mitosis cell division each new cell that is produced is a complete copy of the one it came from. Cells divide in a pattern: **1, 2, 4, 8, 16, 32, 64,** etc.*

The process of cell division

*Over a period of **120** hours a single cell divides many times on its journey to the uterus. There, after about a week, it implants into the lining of the uterus.*

HELPING NATURE

Sometimes natural fertilisation cannot take place because of problems, such as blocked fallopian tubes in the woman or low numbers of sperm in the man. However, modern medicine can often overcome these problems. Eggs can be removed from a woman's ovaries and sperm collected from her partner. The sperm and egg are then mixed in a laboratory so that 'artificial' fertilisation takes place. The fertilised egg can then be placed into the woman's uterus so that it can develop into a baby in the normal way.

Test tube fertilisation
Artificial fertilisation can sometimes help couples who have difficulty making babies.

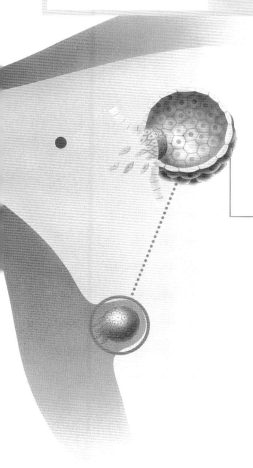

Morula and blastocyst

After about three days the first cell has become a ball of **16** cells called a morula. It is about the size of the head of a pin. After about five days the group of dividing cells reaches the uterus. It has become a hollow ball of cells called a blastocyst. About a week after fertilisation the blastocyst implants in the lining of the uterus. When this happens the blastocyst produces a hormone that signals that pregnancy has started.

Implanted blastocyst
Soon after the blastocyst implants in the lining of the uterus it begins to form an embryo and the placenta.

Placenta and umbilical cord

A group of cells on the inner wall of the blastocyst now start to form an embryo. The cells on the outer walls of the blastocyst help form the placenta – a flat disc of tissue that forms on the wall of the uterus. Inside the placenta blood vessels of the embryo and the mother come close together, but their blood does not mix. This allows food and oxygen to pass from the mother to the developing baby and for carbon dioxide and other wastes to pass from the baby to the mother. The developing baby is attached to the placenta by the umbilical cord.

The baby develops from
an embryo to a foetus

The 38–40 weeks it takes for a ball of cells to become a baby is a time of incredible change. During this time, the embryo grows very rapidly to become a small human being called a foetus, complete in almost every detail. The baby is protected by a sac of amniotic fluid and nourished by the placenta. The growing baby continues to expand the uterus as it reaches maturity.

A foetus

This 3-dimensional ultrasound scan shows a mature foetus. Until it is ready to be born it is protected inside a sac of fluid.

The embryo develops

In the first eight weeks of development the embryo grows rapidly. By four weeks it is about 10,000 times heavier than the fertilised egg from which it developed. During this time cells start to form specific types of tissue — for example muscles, bones and organs. This process is thought to be controlled by the genes in each cell. Eight weeks after fertilisation the embryo is recognisable as a human being and is called a foetus.

From embryo to foetus

*During the first few weeks of the pregnancy the embryo is small when compared to the size of the uterus. During the next **32** weeks it grows and expands the uterus.*

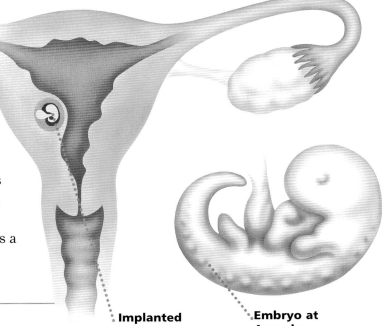

Implanted embryo
is connected to the mother by the placenta

Embryo at 4 weeks
is about 5 millimetres long and is connected to the placenta by the umbilical cord

DEVELOPING BABY

Hospitals and clinics have many tools that can check whether a pregnancy is progressing normally and the foetus is developing properly. One of the most important is the ultrasound machine. This uses high-frequency sound waves that pass through the wall of the uterus. The sound waves bounce off the foetus and this 'echo' is picked up and used to create a picture of the developing baby on a monitor.

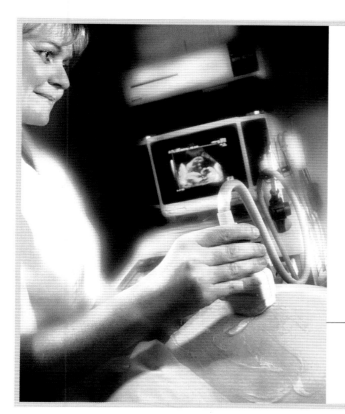

Ultrasound scan

Scans, like the one being performed here, provide the mother with the first glimpse of her unborn baby.

Foetus at 8 weeks is about 3 centimetres long

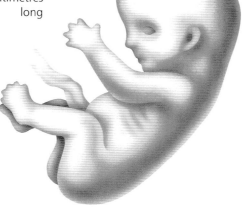

Foetus at 32 weeks

The foetus is nearing maturity and is about 30 centimetres long. It has developed fingers and toes, teeth in its jaw and hair on its head. The foetus also moves around in response to stimuli, such as sounds and touch.

Embryo at 6 weeks is about 2 centimetres long – the brain is developing and tiny limbs become clearly visible.

The foetus develops

By about 20 weeks of the pregnancy, arms, legs and most internal organs are well developed and the mother can feel the foetus moving inside her. In the second half of the pregnancy the foetus increases in weight to about three kilograms. In the final weeks of pregnancy the foetus' brain grows bigger and it starts to become aware of things, such as sounds.

Contractions, birth and afterbirth
are part of labour

A baby is normally ready to be born after about 38–40 weeks. At this point the foetus is said to be 'full term' and normally lies with its head pointing downwards. The birth process – or labour – is started by hormones produced by the baby and placenta. Labour has three main stages: contractions, birth and afterbirth.

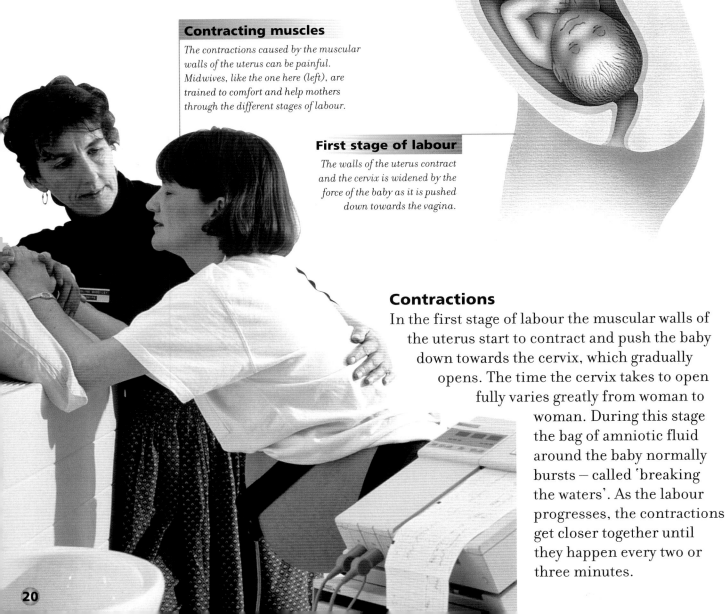

Contracting muscles

The contractions caused by the muscular walls of the uterus can be painful. Midwives, like the one here (left), are trained to comfort and help mothers through the different stages of labour.

First stage of labour

The walls of the uterus contract and the cervix is widened by the force of the baby as it is pushed down towards the vagina.

Contractions

In the first stage of labour the muscular walls of the uterus start to contract and push the baby down towards the cervix, which gradually opens. The time the cervix takes to open fully varies greatly from woman to woman. During this stage the bag of amniotic fluid around the baby normally bursts – called 'breaking the waters'. As the labour progresses, the contractions get closer together until they happen every two or three minutes.

Birth

The second stage of labour is the birth itself, when the baby is pushed out of the uterus through the vagina. This can happen in a few minutes or can take several hours. The head usually comes out first, followed by the shoulders and then the rest of the body. When the baby is delivered, the umbilical cord, which still links it to the placenta inside the mother, is clamped and then cut. In the next few weeks the end of the umbilical cord attached to the baby shrivels and the scar eventually forms the navel or 'bellybutton'.

Afterbirth

Once the baby is born it takes its first breath and normally starts to cry. It is then checked to see that it is healthy and handed to the mother so that she can hold it. The last stage of labour happens when the afterbirth, the placenta and the remainder of the umbilical cord, is expelled from the uterus. This usually takes anywhere from 2–30 minutes.

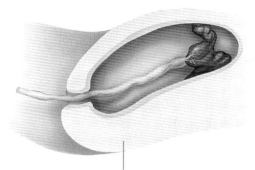

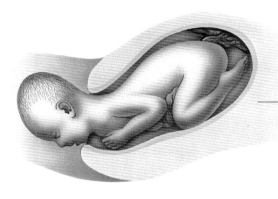

Second stage

Once the cervix has widened fully, the baby is pushed through the vagina. The baby's head turns to allow it to pass between its mother's legs.

Third stage

The uterus continues to contract until the placenta and remainder of the umbilical cord has passed out of the uterus. The labour is now over.

BIRTH CHOICES

The birth of a baby is painful for the mother and many women have some sort of pain relief. This is normally in the form of a pain-killing drug that is either breathed in or injected.

Some women choose to have their babies in hospital, others choose to have their babies at home. In either case, doctors or midwives are normally standing by to help. If a baby cannot be born in a natural way, then it can be delivered by caesarian section. This is an operation in which the baby is delivered through a cut made in the uterus.

A new arrival

The birth of a new baby is a very exciting time for a family. The baby is completely dependent on them for his or her every need.

Twins are the most common type of
multiple birth

When most women become pregnant only one baby develops in their uterus, but some mothers find that they have two, or more, babies inside them. This is called a multiple birth. Twins are the most common kind of multiple birth and occur in about 1 in every 70 to 80 pregnancies. Twins either look the same as each other or are different. These two kinds of twins develop inside the uterus for different reasons and in slightly different ways.

Non-identical twins

In the uterus, non-identical twins live independently of each other. Each baby is joined to a separate placenta.

Non-identical twins

Most twins do not look the same — they are non-identical twins. When they are born they look just like any other brothers or sisters. Non-identical twins are formed if two eggs are released from a woman's ovary at the same time. Different sperm fertilise these eggs. They then go on to develop in the normal way and are joined to the uterus by separate placentas. The two embryos have different selections of their parents' genes and look like a normal brother and sister — except that they are delivered within minutes of each other.

MORE THAN TWO!

While twins are a big surprise for some parents – others have something even more unexpected in store. Women have given birth to six, seven and even eight healthy babies at one time. Multiple births can happen naturally, but many are now occurring because of the use of fertility drugs. These drugs often work by increasing the number of eggs that are released from a woman's ovaries. If these multiple eggs are all fertilised, then the mother develops multiple babies.

Identical twins

Identical twins occur less often than non-identical twins. Identical twins share the same genetic information and therefore look exactly the same and are the same sex as each other. They are formed at an early stage of development after a single fertilised egg divides. However, unlike normal cell division (see page 16) two groups of cells move apart and develop separately. These produce two foetuses.

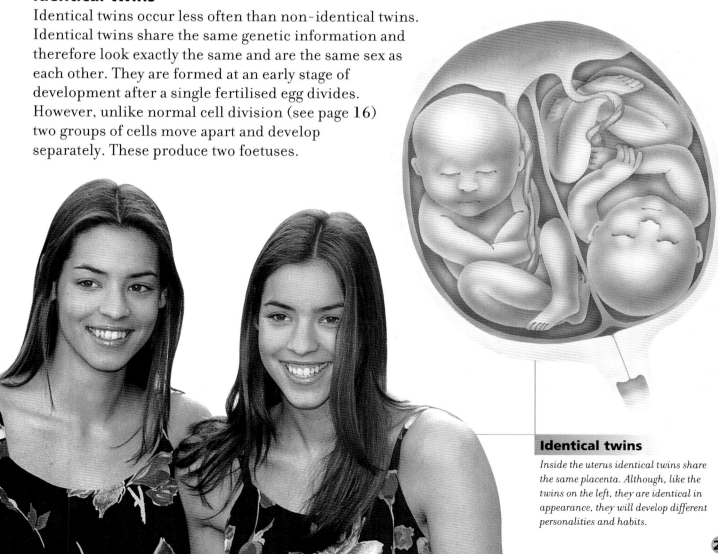

Identical twins

Inside the uterus identical twins share the same placenta. Although, like the twins on the left, they are identical in appearance, they will develop different personalities and habits.

Babies change shape and
grow up quickly

When a baby is born it is completely helpless. As a baby grows to become a child, a teenager and a young adult he or she changes physically, mentally and emotionally and becomes increasingly independent and able to cope on their own.

A liquid start

To begin with babies can only drink milk. This is provided by their mother's breasts or from 'formula' milk in a bottle. As they get older, babies can start to eat other foods and by about one year old they can eat most solid foods. From then on children need to eat a balanced diet that will help them grow properly (see opposite).

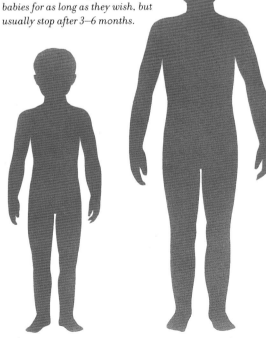

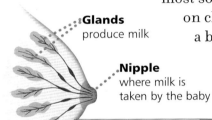

Glands
produce milk

Nipple
where milk is
taken by the baby

Inside a breast

Glands in the breast begin producing milk after the birth. The milk travels along tubes that bunch together at the nipple.

Breast-feeding

Mothers can breast-feed their babies for as long as they wish, but usually stop after 3–6 months.

Changing shape

During its first year (called infancy) a baby's physical growth is very rapid. Through childhood the rate of growth slows until adolescence when there is another growth spurt (see pages 26–27). As people get older the shape of their body changes.

One month
Weight 4.1 kgs

Six months
Weight 7.6 kgs

One year
Weight 10.1 kgs

Two years
Weight 12.6 kgs

Four years
Weight 16.5 kgs

Six years
Weight 21.9 kgs

FOOD FOR GROWTH

Without food and water we cannot live or grow; it is important to eat the right things to stay healthy and grow properly. Many experts advise that we should eat a balanced diet that provides us with the right amounts of carbohydrates, proteins, minerals, vitamins, fibre and fat. We should also try to limit the amount of sugars we take in.

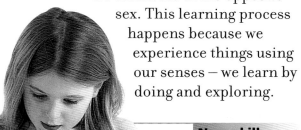

Physical change

*This sequence shows how the shape and average weight of a child's body changes from the age of one month to **10** years.*

A balanced diet

The food we eat affects how we grow, especially during infancy and adolescence.

Learning process

As people grow, they also learn new skills. These skills can be physical, for example a baby learning to walk; mental, for example a child learning to read; or emotional, for example a teenager developing feelings for members of the opposite sex. This learning process happens because we experience things using our senses — we learn by doing and exploring.

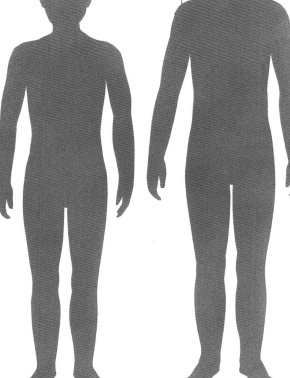

New skills

During childhood (from infancy to adolescence) children develop a wide range of skills including reading, speech and numeracy.

Eight years
Weight 27.3 kgs

Ten years
Weight 32.6 kgs

The reproductive system is activated **during puberty**

One of the most important stages of growing up is called puberty. This usually happens to boys and girls during their teenage, or adolescent, years. Puberty is controlled by chemicals called sex hormones. These hormones cause a person's reproductive system to become fully functional. This means that they are physically able to make children. During puberty boys and girls experience a number of other physical and mental changes, which together turn them from children into young adults.

Emotional change

Puberty is only partly about the physical changes that occur. It is also a time when young adolescents become increasingly independent of their parents and aware of their own individuality.

Reproductive action

One of the most significant changes in girls is the start of their periods (see pages 8–9). This is caused by the release of female sex hormones into the blood and signal that a woman is now ovulating; her reproductive system is active.

The most important change for boys occurs when they start to produce sperm. This usually happens between the ages of **13** and **14,** although it can occur earlier or later. The start of sperm production is caused by male sex hormones.

Growth spurt

During puberty boys and girls grow rapidly. Their body shape changes. Girls become more rounded, boys become more muscular. Boys and girls also develop 'secondary' sexual characteristics. For example, a girl develops breasts and her nipples enlarge. A boy's penis and testes enlarge, his voice 'breaks' and he grows hair on his body and face. Both sexes grow pubic hair around their genitals.

These physical changes are accompanied by mental and 'emotional' development: many boys and girls start to take an interest in the opposite sex. They also become more independent of their parents.

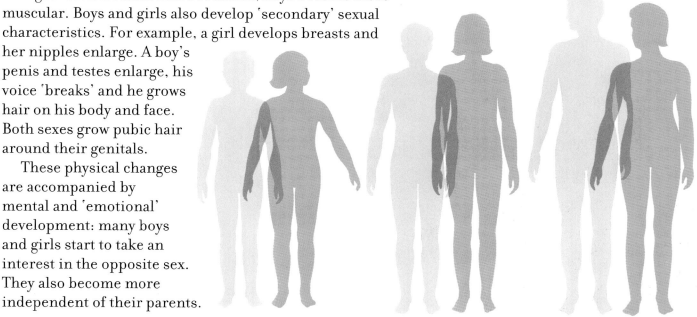

Growing up

Puberty is a time of many changes. Most importantly it is when a boy and girl first become physically able to make children; they become young adults. However, they are not emotionally ready for the demands and responsibilities of parenthood.

Around 11 years
Boys and girls develop pubic hair. Girls' nipples start to enlarge. Boys' muscles develop.

Around 13 years
Boy's penis and testes enlarge, sperm production begins, voice breaks and facial hair may start to grow. Girls start their periods and their hips and breasts continue to develop.

Around 18 years
Boys may grow chest hair, their shoulders get wider and their voice deepens. Girls' hips become rounder and their breasts mature.

SKIN CARE
Many teenagers experience skin problems, such as acne or pimples, when they reach puberty. Acne is normally caused by oil clogging the tiny holes or pores that cover the skin. Acne affects people during puberty because the increase in the sex hormones in the body causes the skin to produce more oil. It is a myth that certain foods, such as chocolate, increase the risk of spots.

Clean living

Most teenagers find that they get spots sooner or later – often when they are least wanted! But by washing properly most people can help to reduce their numbers greatly.

The body continues to change
in adulthood

Men and women grow to their full height in their late teens, but the body never really stops changing. Gradually, as we move into adulthood and get older, more noticeable changes begin to take place as the body starts to age or wear out. Other changes can occur as a result of illness or an accident. Living a healthy lifestyle can reduce the impact of ageing and many old people live full and active lives. Eventually, however, everyone's life comes to an end and they die.

Old and wrinkly

We change in different ways over a period of time as we get older. For many people the main sign of ageing is the development of wrinkly skin, like this woman's.

Noticeable effects

The process of ageing occurs over a long period of time, but by the time someone is 45–55 years old the effects can be seen clearly. For example, older people get wrinkles on their skin as it loses its elasticity and sags. Hair begins to turn grey because the cells that create the colour in the hair die gradually. Many older people also shrink because their bones begin to deteriorate. A major change for women happens when, after about the age of 50, they stop being able to have babies. This is called the menopause.

Prone to illness

As people get older they also become more likely to be affected by certain illnesses, such as cancer, arthritis, Alzheimer's disease and heart disease. Many factors can make the symptoms of ageing worse and make people more likely to fall ill. These include smoking, unhealthy eating, poor living conditions and unreliable health care.

WHEN ARE YOU OLD?

'Getting old' means different things at different times in a person's life. Leaving school or celebrating their 40th birthday are things that make people feel they are getting old, but as long as people stay healthy they can lead a full, active life.

People retire from their full-time jobs when they are older. Many take the opportunity offered by the extra free time they have to travel and take up new interests and hobbies.

Getting old

Many people spend more time with their family as they get older.

Natural ending

Regular exercise, a healthy diet and a positive approach to life can all help older people keep healthy and active. However, everyone dies eventually. Women in general live about seven years longer than men, although the average age of death varies around the world. In places where most people have a high standard of living, such as Western Europe, many people live beyond their **80**s. In places where life is harder, such as Africa, many people die long before this.

Life expectancy

*The age of death in some countries, such as Uganda in East Africa, is much lower than in many other parts of the world. Younger members of this family would not expect to live much past the age of **50**.*

Glossary

Amniotic fluid The fluid that surrounds and protects the developing baby inside the uterus.

Blastocyst The hollow ball of cells that develops about five days after fertilisation and from which an embryo and the placenta develop.

Chromosomes Thread-like structures inside the nucleus of a cell that carry genes.

Contraception A drug, method or device that stops a woman becoming pregnant.

Egg The female sex cell, produced by the ovary.

Embryo The early stage of the development of a baby. After eight weeks the developing baby is called a foetus.

Epididymis A long coiled tube in which sperm mature after they are made in the testes.

Fallopian tube One of a pair of tubes that carry eggs from the ovaries to the uterus.

Fertilisation The fusing together of a sperm and an egg to produce a fertilised egg. This egg develops into a new baby.

Foetus The stage of the development of a baby from eight weeks after fertilisation until birth.

Follicle A bag of cells inside an ovary that surrounds and nourishes a maturing egg.

Genes The chemical code carried on chromosomes. Genes contain instructions for how a person should look and function. Genes are inherited from parents.

Hormones Chemical messengers produced by the body. Hormones control many things that happen in the body, including the development of sexual organs and reproduction.

Implantation When a fertilised egg attaches itself to the lining of the uterus.

Labour The process by which a baby is born.

Menstrual cycle A sequence of changes that repeat every month and prepare a woman's body for pregnancy. The cycle involves the release of an egg from an ovary and the loss and renewal of the lining of the uterus.

Menstruation (also called 'a period') The loss of blood and tissue through the vagina that happens when the lining of the uterus is shed during the menstrual cycle.

Morula The solid mass of dividing cells that develops in the first few days after an egg has been fertilised.

Nucleus The central part of a cell that contains the chromosomes.

Ovaries A pair of organs that release eggs.

Ovulation The release of an egg from an ovary.

Penis The part of the male reproductive system used to transfer sperm into a woman's vagina during sexual intercourse.

Period See menstruation.

Placenta The organ that links (but does not combine) the blood supply of the developing baby to the blood supply of its mother.

Pregnancy The time between conception and birth, during which a new baby develops and grows in the uterus.

Prostate gland A gland that adds fluid to sperm during ejaculation.

Puberty The stage in a person's life when their sex organs mature and they become able to reproduce.

Scrotum A bag of skin that contains the testes.

Semen The fluid produced during ejaculation containing sperm and secretions from various glands.

Sex cells The sperm and eggs.

Sex chromosomes The pair of chromosomes that determines the sex of a person.

Sex hormones Hormones produced by the ovary and testes that control sexual function and behaviour.

Sexual intercourse When a man puts his penis inside a woman's vagina and sperm is released.

Sperm Male sex cells, produced in the testes.

Testes A pair of organs that produce sperm.

Umbilical cord The tube-like structure that connects the developing baby and the placenta.

Uterus The hollow muscular organ in which a baby develops. (Also called the womb.)

Vagina A muscular tube that links the uterus to the outside of the body.

Find out more

These are just some of the websites where you can find out more information about the human lifecycle. Many of the websites also provide information and illustrations about other systems and processes of the human body.

Note to parents and teachers
Every effort has been made by the Publishers to ensure that these websites are suitable for children; that they are of the highest educational value, and that they contain no inappropriate or offensive material. However, because of the nature of the Internet, it is impossible to guarantee that the contents of these sites will not be altered. We strongly advise that Internet access is supervised by a responsible adult.

www.howstuffworks.com
Go to the 'science stuff' section of this site for information on how reproduction and genes work.

www.bbc.co.uk/science/humanbody
A website devoted to the parts of the body and how they work – check out the interactive body demonstration of what happens during puberty.

www.brainpop.com/health
Find out all about where babies come from, including information on fertilisation, growth and birth. You can even download animated movies which will show you how everything works.

www.galaxy-h.gov.uk
This website covers a range of personal, social and health education topics.

www.kidshealth.org
Loads of information about reproduction and growing up – if you have got a question, you should find an answer here.

www.innerbody.com
A great site to find out about all the different parts that make up the male and female reproductive systems, along with all the other bits of the body.

www.ajkids.com
A search engine for asking questions about science – just type in your query, press return and you will be shown where to get the best answer.

www.lifebytes.gov.uk
A website for older children that provides lots of information about growing up and dealing with new feelings.

www.cyh.com/cyh/kids
The website of the Australian Child and Youth Health Unit that aims to help you 'start healthy and stay healthy'. It provides lots of information about your body and advice for coping with your feelings.

www.abc.net.au/talkitup
This website for older children is dedicated to issues about health, happiness and growing up. It aims to help you acquire new skills for dealing with the physical and emotional changes ahead.

Index